YOU HAVE TO LAUGH

YOU HAVE TO LAUGH

Riffs on Aging

By Susan Evans

SMALL BATCH BOOKS
AMHERST, MASSACHUSETTS

Printed in the United States of America

Design by Megan Katsanevakis

ISBN: 978-1-951568-42-9

SMALL
BATCH
BOOKS

493 SOUTH PLEASANT STREET
AMHERST, MASSACHUSETTS 01002
413.230.3943
smallbatchbooks.com

*To Shell,
my partner in life and aging.
Thanks for having the grace to be one day older
than I am and for seeing me through the good times
and the bad.*

Contents

OPTION TO RENEW

In my fifties and sixties I thumbed my nose at aging. "I just want to get to eighty with everything in working order and an option to renew," I would jest. Implicit in the mirth, of course, was that everything *would* be in working order. I was realistic about the fact that I would die someday, but extremely unrealistic about the fact that I would get older in the process.

I'm currently less than a year away from that magic number, and the picture looks quite different from this perspective. My best friend and role model, who is conveniently four years older than I am and thus breaking trail for me, warned that when I turned seventy, every year would bring unexpected challenges. I hadn't experienced much decline in my sixties, so I smugly discounted her forecast. At first the changes were subtle—a stiff back in the morning, increasing the size of the print on my Kindle ever so slightly with each new book, turning up the volume on the car radio—changes I could almost ignore. Around age seventy-two, though, I began to see ugly dark splotches every time I bumped myself even slightly, a condition my GP wrote off as "to be expected," and I knew I had inadvertently crept into "old age." What a comeuppance.

I won't go into the litany of issues I'm dealing with in my seventy-ninth year, as I find the "organ recital," as my fellow geezers call it, to be boring, even when it's about me. Suffice it to say, it's a long, if manageable, list so far. And . . . I'm doing pretty well for my age, although I try to keep that observation to myself, lest my children roll their eyeballs at me the way I did when my mother used that phrase. I knew she was fishing for compliments, and I withheld them—one of the many regrets I have to live with about my relationship with my mom. Maybe my children will read this and be able to avoid that regret. They'll have plenty of others.

The clock is ticking inexorably, and that all-important eighty-year deadline looms. It's no longer an issue for jest. I'm humbled by the challenges of aging and in awe of the people who are dealing with problems considerably more severe than my own. I'm skeptical of prayer, but desperate times call for desperate measures, so I ask for strength and grit (and, not incidentally, all my marbles) on a daily basis. If a child of mine is in earshot, I also throw in "Forgive us our foibles" so they know we old folks don't mean to be annoying. I will definitely sign the option to renew if proffered, and I no longer take that for granted. I know I'm one of the lucky ones.

STOP ME

If you catch yourself saying, "Stop me if I've already told you this . . . ," trust me, you have. Some stories are just so delicious, they deserve to be retold, though, right? Who wouldn't respond positively—laugh out loud, or at least smile—at my retelling of Luke skiing backward into the side of an outhouse when he was in ski school at the age of five? It only gets funnier the older and bigger he gets—or so I think as I launch into it with overly animated glee and the occasional new detail. So, okay, I know the answer to the question before I even open my mouth, but I just can't help myself. I'm having a good time, even if no one else is.

Seniors are tarred and feathered with being over re-peaters, but I've listened to my son gas on about the plays he ran as a flag football coach, and I can mouth the words to the story my (younger) friend Karen tells about the time Bruce Springsteen plucked her onstage at a concert. Clearly it is a failing not limited to seniors—just viewed as more unattractive in our age group, unless you are George Burns, of course. It's human nature to want to share your special moments. The problem seems to be the lack of new and interesting material we elderly possess. There's the ninety-seven-year-old who trained to crest Kilimanjaro by running the seventeen floors of his assisted-living facility, and the grandmother who has written three historical novels starting in her eighties, but they're outliers. The bulk of us have only arthritic knees and cataracts to wax on about, hardly the makings of compelling sagas.

What to do? My latest ploy is to recount an escapade from the current book I'm reading.

"Did you hear about the woman who discovered her father wasn't her biological dad through Ancestry.com? Both of her adoptive parents were dead, so she had no way to question them and had to go on an involved search for her real father. What do you think *you* would do in that situation?"

Or bring up a topic from the news, though you have to vet your audience carefully in today's fraught political scene. While you might not leave your listener hanging on your every word, you will at least have planted the seed that your mind might still be working.

I wrote a family history full of amusing (you will have to trust me on that) anecdotes about my ancestors. Since none of my relatives have commented on it, I assume it has gone unread. If they aren't interested in their own genes, they can hardly want to hear about the time I charmed the cop out of giving me a speeding ticket. Which brings me to what I think is the crux of the matter. Most people would rather tell their own tales than listen to one of mine. I have a lovely daughter-in-law who's an Olympic-class listener and, as a result, hears about more sins than the Pope, but she's unusual. The mindfulness coaches warn us not to think about our rejoinder when someone else is speaking, but in my experience, their advice is falling on deaf ears. My closest friend of thirty-plus years reliably launches into her account way before I have come to the point of mine. My story seems to just be a jumping-off point for hers. In fairness, my tale might not be brand-new to her either. When caught in a repeat, I'm forced to wonder, *Is this a senior moment or the start of something more serious? Something to laugh off or something to lose sleep over?* My older readers will relate.

Writing personal essays is a cathartic experience, and this piece has done its job by lightening my load. Retelling stories is a universal sin and done with the best of intentions, the desire to share and connect. The trick, then, becomes finding new audiences for old tales. I'm fairly sure my book group hasn't heard the story about Luke and the outhouse. I know they're going to love it.

THE INEVITABLE

Many moons ago my husband and I were at dinner with our mothers when they were about the age we are now. They flanked my husband and peppered him with asides.

"How old is she, really?" my mother barked. She was extremely hard of hearing, and if you don't know enough old people to know that the less you hear, the louder you speak, you do now.

"She can't hear a thing," my husband's mother observed.

"She's a little unsteady," my mother suggested, "which must be why she's in assisted living."

We howled like hyenas at the competitive nature of the two old crones, but I now have a better idea of the rationale behind it. One of my guilty pleasures is standing in the pickup line at the CVS pharmacy and straining to hear the birth date of the person fortunate enough to have reached the counter. Is he/she older or younger than me? Better preserved? More nimble? Navigating independently?

We have decamped to Florida, where gray hair is the norm, so I'm usually pretty pleased with my place in the pecking order but should be embarrassed by the need to compare. I'm not. I'm still cognizant enough to remember every detail about the girls in seventh grade and how I measured up. Same difference.

I'm told I no longer need colonoscopies on the theory that at my age, tumors would grow so slowly, they wouldn't be life-threatening. Initially, I was gleeful. The blueberry muffin the nurses offered as a reward at the end is not enough lure to continue the prep. On closer examination, though, I realized that if a tumor would be slow growing, so would everything else, including my nails and hair. I could live (interesting verb choice) with the idea that my nose is no longer growing, but nails and hair? I'm still vain enough to care about them . . . which leads to a major issue for the aging population.

When do you succumb to the inevitable?

I've been a dedicated—obsessive, some would contend— exerciser for most of my adult life.

"It isn't going to make you live any longer," my ever-supportive and, I suspect, slightly jealous mother used to observe.

"Maybe not, Ma, but I'll feel better along the way."

It's proven to be true. It started out for vanity (those pesky last pounds) but has continued for sanity. Best tranquilizer on the planet. But I digress.

Back to the inevitable. I quit skiing ten years ago, quit crewing on a large sailboat five. I still power walk and go to the gym in order to be able to play an hour of geriatric tennis three times a week but find myself watching the clock on the court to make sure we don't run overtime.

"I can't afford to fall," I whine as an excuse for cutting back.

My extraordinarily fit—and older—brother-in-law-suggested to me that the key to aging well was to stay injury-free. When he quit skiing, I did too. Ten fractures to my name were a powerful motivator, but so was the thought of a broken hip. I was recently leaving a lady's luncheon of my peers and noticed that most of us were sporting kitten heels, if there were any heels at all, and every one of us grabbed the railing before we braved the stairs—an instinctive act of self-preservation.

The physical limitations are obvious: not being able to open a childproof cap, needing glasses to chop onions so that you don't lose a digit, making sure the good-looking man sits on your right side at dinner so that you can actually hear him instead of just nodding knowingly. The mental ones are more nuanced and ten times scarier. A former surgeon general told our group at a health retreat that the fear of dementia had far surpassed the fear of cancer and heart disease in our age bracket. But we knew that.

For the distaff side, it starts with perimenopause, when forgetfulness can be excused as hormonal. As time marches on, though, those brain farts that are initially written off as senior moments to make them seem benign become more commonplace. One is left to ponder, often at 3:00 a.m., *How much memory loss is normal?*

Recently I was plagued by a song playing relentlessly in my head as I was trying to go to sleep. I could remember the name of the song, could picture the album cover, remembered seeing the artist in concert, the friends we were with that night, but damn if I could remember her name. Sleep became impossible as I went through my mental rock-and-roll Rolodex until I came up with the idea of going through the alphabet to see if one of the letters would jog my memory. It took a couple of runs, but I finally came up with Kathy Mattea. I was chuffed about my clever technique but so wide awake, I had to grab the Kindle I keep on my bedside table for insomnia emergencies. Was this an acceptable lapse? Nothing to worry about? Or . . . *dah-dum, dah-dum* . . . the beginning of serious decline?

I've read that the major contributor to memory loss is distraction, and that we elderly are more prone to distraction than our younger counterparts. I would contend that my teenage grandson, who has a speeding ticket, a fender bender, and left half of his gear at home when he left for college, is competitive. With him, we indulgently say he's absent-minded. When I have a wee incident backing into another car in the parking lot (in my defense, no backup camera since the car is almost as old as I am), the family court suggests—and not indulgently, I would add—that maybe it's time to take my keys away.

They aren't entirely wrong. Science suggests shortened telomeres, frayed synapses. Whatever the cause, the compromised attention span of us oldsters is real. Never a particularly adept driver, I have turned off the car radio in an attempt to increase my awareness. I know my reaction speed and spatial sense aren't what they used to be (which never were all that reliable, truth be told), so I try to give myself and my fellow road mates every chance. An unexpected consequence of silent driving, though, is that my lifelong earworm has subsided now that I'm no longer barraged by oldies. Since I'm not singing along to "Wake Up Little Susie," I spend the time worrying about my younger grandson getting injured playing football and whether my granddaughter will get into her first choice of schools. In other words, I'm just as distracted, which indicates it comes with the territory.

Long before we slid into the mislabeled golden years, my husband observed that "The older we get, the more like ourselves we become." I found that extremely insightful the first time he said it but am finding it a bit wearing with repetition.

Who among us doesn't repeat stories? I don't, of course, but I seem to be an outlier. My ears fold up when my husband recounts yet again that he played Eeyore to Michael Douglas's Christopher Robin in their middle school play. He isn't the only one of my cadre of peers whose amusing anecdotes I can repeat verbatim, but he's the one I have to indulge the most often. After serious contemplation and accusations from my son that I repeat myself, too (really?), I've concluded that the reason we revisit old memories so often is that we aren't making new ones. I struggle to remember the last time I did something worth adding to my repertoire of escapades. As it is, I look back and wonder, *Who was that woman?*

I haven't answered the question about succumbing to the inevitable but, rather, have rambled on, another trademark sin of my age group. I would like to believe I've made appropriate concessions to old age by retiring from skiing and sailing, but in most cases the concessions have been forced on me. The kids laugh when I ask for help opening a jar of jam or, more often, a bottle of champagne, but I get the last laugh reminding myself . . . it will happen to them too. I'm sorry I won't be around to see it.

CRINGEY

We oldsters are an unattractive lot. Think thinning hair, not-so-white teeth, arthritic hands. The best that can be said about us individually is that we look "pretty good for our age." Talk about damning with faint praise. My grandsons refer to us as "cringey," a blanket expression for how embarrassing we older people are to the younger generation . . . particularly teenagers

Cringey feels harsh. I could accept "unseemly" or "unbecoming," as long as it was modified with "a little," but cringey takes it too far. After all, we don't mean to be. But . . . some days you just don't see the tiny dab of salsa that landed on your left boob until you do the laundry, and you're guilty as charged.

My grandmother lived with us for three months in

the winter, and while I was glued to her side when we were at home, I was careful to distance myself in public. My grandmother seemed born old. I couldn't imagine a younger version, which is pretty much the way I suspect our grandchildren view us. I confess I'm in the habit of keeping large pictures of us in our prime around the house and blatantly pointing them out.

"There's your grandfather sailing in the Bermuda race," I remark in a manner I hope is breezy enough not to sound calculated.

"That's me with brown hair. Remember?"

A rhetorical question if there ever was one. *I* barely remember me with brown hair. Of course they don't. They will remember us, if they do at all, as gray haired and crepey. They will remember their grandfather's gravelly voice and my knee braces. They will remember that Grampy takes a nap after lunch and that we both go to bed before they do. They will remember us as old.

I fight it with a vigor my spouse finds misplaced.

"You look fine," he declares as he scrolls through his emails.

His powers of observation lost their cred years ago when he failed to notice I'd gotten a tattoo until someone else pointed it out. It's discreet, I admit, but still.

Covid forced me to go gray, but I'm hanging on to what hair I still have with a regimen of Rogaine and a laser cap that stimulates the roots three days a week. Oh, and a supplement with questionable benefits, but so far my hair is full, if not exactly bushy, so why stop? It goes without saying that I wear sunscreen, even in the dead of winter, and have fortunately discovered the tinted kind that looks like I'm wearing foundation. Once I've created a flawless complexion, I might as well highlight the eyes and splash on some blush. You get the picture.

The trickiest part is the wardrobe. There's a fine line between dowdy and trying too hard, and it's a minefield. Short, ruffled skirts are obviously out, but what about a cute frilly blouse? The mothers wearing thongs at my local pool are a stern reminder that trying to look young is in fact aging—extremely so in some cases. I only wear my cutoff jeans in the garden and have given away my collection of tank tops, but it leaves me with a limited closet full of tailored pants and long-sleeved tees. They make me look invisible, but at least not blatantly cringey.

My mother did a masterful job of looking pulled to-gether well into her eighties, when she fell (or perhaps jumped—my mother was large and in charge till the bitter end) into the abyss. Seemingly overnight, she gave up chic Anne Klein outfits for the kind of all-elasticized wardrobe one usually associates with plus sizes. She also gave up wearing shoes despite a collection that would have caused Sarah Jessica Parker a twinge of envy. The result was undeniably cringey, as she could no longer reach her toes and had been banned from the local nail spa. I sensed she didn't care.

On one memorable trip when I was staying at her house, I was shopping in the local A&P when a woman flew in on a motorized scooter. She was cruising well above the speed limit, and—gasp—she wasn't wearing shoes. Her outfit was a bit of a blur since she was going so fast, but I immediately recognized the helmet-like haircut. "Step aside," she telegraphed, and I complied. I recognized her but didn't have the courage to call out. She looked like someone whose kids had abandoned her.

My mother has been a positive role model in many ways, but I hope to avoid leaving my blood relatives with an indelible memory such as the above. My husband, who has given up combing his hair except for special occasions, says that I'm kidding myself. Entropy coupled with the fatigue endemic to old age always wins, he contends. Maybe so, but I'm not willing to concede just yet.

My watch just pinged. Time to take off the teeth whiteners.

FUNERALS AND OBITS

Now that funerals have replaced weddings and baptisms as the mainstay of my social life, I've developed some strong opinions about my own. I would prefer to not need one, of course, but think I'd better cover my bases just in case. I've been to some lovely services in church, but Jesus always seems to grab center stage, and selfishly, I want this to be about me. I attended a moving memorial for an offshore fisherman in the local watering hole (sorry, but that expression was too good to pass up), where there was an open mic and people randomly shared memories. It got a bit raucous, which was appropriate for the deceased, but I want something a bit more decorous. Given how distraught I expect my family will be, I can leave nothing to chance. In fact, I better put a deposit down on the hall now and arrange for sunflowers so that all they will have to do is order food. They already know they will be serving champagne, as it has been my lifelong drug of choice, but they'll have to shop around for a cheaper version of my usual quaff, as I expect the crowds will be staggering.

Now that the stage is set, I think the festivities should start out with a poem. Something to get the emotions amped up. I'm thinking of Wordsworth:

Though nothing can bring back the hour
Of splendour in the grass, of glory in the flower;
We will grieve not, rather find
Strength in what remains behind

That should get them properly emotional.

Next I would like brief—and I do mean brief—reminiscences from my children. How many eulogists lose their audience—and, not incidentally, the point of their speech—by droning on? I'm hopeful that some of the grandchildren I have so outrageously indulged will be moved to speak about my positive influence on their lives, but I realize they might get stage fright in front of such a large audience. They're exempt. Certain friends—and you know who you are—are not. I'll leave it to my husband to close by leaving the house in tears. It sounds so appealing, I'm sorry I'll have to miss it. I realize there are those who do celebrate their passing in advance, but I think that's a bit showy, even for me.

My family is fairly STEM-centric, so I better write the obituary myself. They would just stick to the facts, and my life deserves some color. I had a friend in my early thirties who introduced me to the prurient joys of reading obits, and as a result, I'm well versed in what works and what doesn't. In my youth, obits were fairly dry affairs mainly listing the deceased's work experience, schools attended, club affiliations (as if that was some kind of achievement), and survivors. They also usually included a cause of death, which I found useful as a gauge to whether I might be vulnerable at the same age. In the internet era, when everyone can Google your dental records, people have become surprisingly coy about revealing cause of death. It no longer has the power to sting the deceased, so why not satisfy the question that everyone (it can't only be me) must be asking.

On the plus side, I embrace the current trend to humanize the person with details like he created stained-glass mobiles in his retirement, or she was devoted to her cats. I am also in favor of including photographs—those are always the ones I read first. It's a hard call whether to include a photo from an earlier date, when the person presumably looked good, or a more realistic, recent one. I think I might opt for my high school yearbook picture, as it should garner the most attention. If I'm going to write an opus, I want it to be read.

I think that takes care of it. If I'm ever advised to go home and put my affairs in order, I will be able to put on a smug smile and crow ... "I already have."

———

OBITUARY
Susan Carkhuff Evans (1944-2????)

Susan Carkhuff Evans was born on March 21, 1944, which her mother contended was the first day of spring and, thus, a positive omen. Like the beginning of the season, she arrived amid sunshine and high hopes. She was fortunate to grow up in post-WWII Pax Americana, where children feasted on sugarcoated cereal and rode bikes without helmets. She cruised with a neighborhood gang and had no need for "play dates." Her education prepared her to be whatever she wanted to be but subtly implied her best use was as a wife and mother, so, like most of her peers, that became her career path. Also like most of her peers, she was heavily involved in volunteer work, participating in everything from organizing the ever-popular balloon race for her children's school to teaching English as a second language to refugees from Haiti. She found her niche facilitating groups of bereaved parents after the death of her daughter, Courtney, and served at the Den for Grieving Kids for more than twenty-five years. Her crowning achievement was helping to create a viable and supportive stepfamily. In addition to her son, Michael Robinson, she leaves behind her stepchildren, Ashley MacDonald and Jonathan Evans, whom she never liked introducing as "steps," as the term didn't adequately describe the relationship. She also leaves behind her husband, Shell, of forty-plus years, who became her sidekick in fifth grade and many iterations later, her soulmate. She adored her seven grandchildren, each of whom enhanced her life in their own unique way. Every Christmas she presented them with a Life is Good T-shirt to remind them—and herself—how truly good their lives were. Her own drawers were full of them as a reminder of her favorite mantra:

Carpe diem.

HOW DO I STACK UP?

I think about my mother all the time. When did she start to lose her hearing? How old was she when she quit driving? What prompted her to let her hair go gray? She's my benchmark, the standard I use to gauge how I'm faring in my golden years.

She was famous for exclaiming, "I'm doing pretty well for my age, you know." And she was. I'm ashamed to admit that I want to do better. What does it say about me that I'm competing with my long-gone mother in a losing battle?

Don't answer that.

I remember my sister and I giggling behind my mother's back when she would complain about one of her friends.

"Liz can't see beyond the end of her nose," she would sniff. "Margie can't hold her booze anymore."

Implicit in these observations was that she still could see an oncoming car a mile away and had not lost her legendary powers of consumption. It was also understood that we were meant to agree with her, a satisfaction my siblings and I rarely extended, a petty slight I now regret. We were woefully ignorant about the challenges of aging and instead scoffed at her lifelong need to be top dog and withheld the affirmation she so desperately craved.

I get it now. My son, who is basically kind and supportive, has the power to decimate me with even a slight suggestion that I'm not my old self.

"Ma," (or more often "Susan," which I guess is to remind me that I'm no longer the omnipotent parent), "you should write down the instructions for the remote so you don't need to call me every time you hit a snag."

"I suggest you Uber to Luke's game. There may not be parking." Code for "You're a liability behind the wheel."

Or my personal favorite, "Haven't I heard that before?"

What goes around comes around, and I'm now doing penance for having infantilized my mom. In fairness to me, she was almost stone deaf, which made communication comical but frustrating. In her dotage she took to sleeping until 10:00, eating breakfast at 11:00, and then eviscerating me for wanting to take her to lunch at 12:30, a reasonable hour for the majority of the world but not her. When she could still drive, she kept a salt shaker in her car for the hard-boiled eggs she was reduced to eating because most restaurants were closed by the time she was ready for lunch. In her mind the world was out of step, not her, and since I was of the world, the problem was me.

As I remember, she was functioning independently until she was ninety. We took her to Alaska when she was eighty-five, which she managed, as we were on a boat and she never had to get off. I have fond memories of her holding court in the lounge, where each of her grandchildren could sit close to her best ear and recount their daily adventures. She would often respond to a story about catching a fish with an observation that the soup for lunch hadn't been very tasty, but we were used to those non sequiturs and knew that it was the contact that was important, not the content.

The summer after Alaska, she bailed on attending her youngest grandchild's wedding, an event I know she would have moved heaven and earth to attend if she could. She had made the trip to California for her only granddaughter's wedding just six months earlier but was no longer mobile enough to navigate this one. The cortisone shots that had been keeping her moving were no longer effective, and she was tired. We knew she could no longer hop on a plane to see us, so we increased our visits to her.

I wish I could say those trips were fun and full of loving moments. I wish we had all had more patience and perspective and adjusted ourselves to her life rather than trying to drag her into ours. There were some lovely moments when we cooked Thanksgiving dinner in her kitchen and had our traditional family football game on her front lawn so that she could watch. And there were the wild rides the great-grands liked to take on her scooter or up the stairs on her elevator seat. But it was frustrating to deflect the repeated "Whats," and as she became increasingly bedridden and unable to properly shower, it was uncomfortable to hang out in her room. She became somewhat spooky to the great-grands, and their visits became commensurately short. Many days my sister and I were the only ones to brave the ninety-degree heat and questionable odors. We talked about the old days and reminisced about ancient parties. Conversation was disjointed, dispirited. She wasn't sad, exactly, but she wasn't entirely engaged either.

"How long do you think I have to live?" she blurted out one afternoon, a question so out of character it caught me flat-footed.

"Who knows?" I awkwardly rejoined, unprepared to address her anxiety. She let it lie and went back to stuffing her poodle companion with treats. We never approached it again.

I know I let her down, but even if I had seen it coming, I wouldn't have known what to say. It's certainly the universal question as we get up in years, but one with no realistic answer. Still, I should have ginned up something soothing, something to calm the fear behind the question. Even now, though, I don't know what that might have been.

"I hear your concern" sounds like psychobabble.

"You must be afraid" sounds patronizing.

Both were probably true, but I doubt would have been helpful. When I try to put myself in her shoes, I can't imagine what it would be like. I'm still at a point in my life where I'm moving ahead—even if not too speedily—and have things to look forward to. While she pretended to be excited about our visits, I think they were stressful. Days before she died, she sent my sister abruptly home. I came soon after in response to a call from her doctor that hospice should be called in. I think she recognized me, but I'm not entirely sure. This was my first brush with death, and I handled it badly. I held her hand and whispered that I loved her but provided no more comfort than I had with her question. I busied myself filling a water glass she no longer needed and taking her dog for walks. I wasn't in the room when she died.

I'll do a better job if put in a similar position again—be more present and attentive. I'm not sure it will make a difference to the person, but I know it will make a difference to me.

TIME-CONSUMING

No wonder we seniors take naps. I'm ready to go back to bed just getting out of it in the morning. By the time I've done my pelvic tilts to loosen up my back, massaged my arthritic fingers, and racked my brain for new things to be grateful for, I'm a touch tired. And ... the maintenance has just begun. I weigh myself, slather my skin with bear grease (the gooiest ointment CVS has to offer), dab Rogaine on my thinning locks, and take the first round of supplements for the day—magnesium to ward off leg cramps and GastroMend to soothe my stomach for the onslaught of the other meds to come. You get the drift. Then there are still my stretches to get through, the mandatory brisk walk, the nutritious breakfast to make, the Wordle to solve. By lunchtime I'm sagging.

I hear my mother from what seems to be her ethereal perch on my left shoulder (my good ear).

"None of that's going to make you any younger, Susan."

I know, but I'm not pursuing youth, Ma. This is strictly self-preservation. If I don't do my back stretches, I can't move. Without the bear grease, my skin itches like I've been swarmed by mosquitoes. And the Rogaine. Well, I'm sure you remember that your mother was bald, so I make no apologies. I don't find bald men all that sexy. On women, it's even less so.

Time is a precious commodity in our later years. We don't want to waste it, and there never seems to be enough. I used to be able to do a load of laundry while I prepped dinner and answered a few phones calls—on a landline, no less. How quaint. Now each activity has to be tackled on its own, lest I mix the whites with the colors, throw the onions for the stew in the cake batter, or leave a message for my son that I'll meet him on Tuesday when we're scheduled for Thursday. The latter would keep me on dementia alert for months.

"Where has the time gone?" is a refrain endemic to those of us running out of it. While the question is usually asked rhetorically, there is a scientific explanation called "log time." A year for a five-year-old is one-fifth of their life so far, but a year for a fifty-year-old is one-fiftieth, so it seems to pass five times faster. A year becomes a smaller fraction of our life the older we get. Do the math. Those of us nearing eighty feel like we're living on fast-forward. Time takes on a sense of urgency just as we are slowing down physically and mentally and thus unable to do anything about it. I had a hard time understanding irony in Freshman Lit. Life hadn't been all that ironic at eighteen. I certainly get it now. *Tempus fugit* . . . and I don't feel up to the task.

"Make every day count," Oprah and her minions exhort. I really do try, but being old is a rather full-time job in itself that leaves little spare time for side gigs. Nevertheless, a worthy goal. After my nap, I think I'll clean out the fridge.

NO JOKE

Before we go any further, let's get something straight. I do know the challenges and fears surrounding aging are real and not something to take lightly. But—and it's a big one—there is usually more than one way to view a situation. I know I'm drifting into preachy territory, but look how well that's worked out for Oprah. The two most upbeat people I know—both women, which I'm sure is merely coincidental—are also the two people who are facing the biggest challenges.

My sister has had numerous compromising falls. Oh yes, and breast cancer, vertigo, and double vision that can't be cured. She has also had bouts of fairly severe depression since she was an adolescent. She's gone from being an accomplished, let me be right behind the master of the hounds horsewoman to a woman who is looking at physical therapy for the rest of her life in order to keep her left hand from atrophying and wearing prism glasses so that she doesn't see two of everything. When I call her, she wants to talk about her dinner plate dahlias, not the fact that she will be a line caller at the mixed-doubles tennis finals and not a contender.

My friend Dedee has COPD as a result of many incidents of childhood pneumonia, which made her a mask wearer long before Covid-19 forced the rest of us to adopt her style. While she has it under control, she fears she might predecease her husband, who has had early-onset dementia for eighteen years. Eighteen years! The time from birth to the end of adolescence. Or from the youth of thirty to the impending middle age of forty-eight. While she occasionally mentions that Jerry is slipping, she usually focuses on how well he can converse about his years at Princeton or the fact that he can still crack up his pals with his wit. When I call her, she often has to put down the phone because she's coughing from what she calls a "wee bout of bronchitis" . . . but then launches into a rapturous description of the snow outside her kitchen window, a substance that rarely moves me to those heights.

Then there is Polly, extolling the fun of hand, knee, and foot canasta now that she can no longer climb mountains; Katie, who taught herself to play tennis with her left hand when she lost the use of her right arm; and Carole, who takes to the dance floor in a wheelchair at weddings. Not everyone is capable of these heroic adaptations, but most of us can at least make an effort.

As warned, this is preachy territory, but these women are worthy of emulation. Their positivity takes effort, but as a result, their glass is always half full. They make sure to refill it.

Enough said. You just need to know I'm not making fun of aging, rather trying to find the fun in the process.

CLICHÉS

I detest clichés. Not because they're corny, though that's true too. I hate the kernel of truth you're forced to acknowledge while you groan, particularly when it pertains to aging. We're supposed to smile and quit complaining when someone points out that "You're only as old as you feel," right? Even on my perkiest of days, that's somewhere north of sixty-five and, frankly, deserving of some whining. But that's the underlying point of all these expressions. They're mini pep talks, meant to suggest that we look on the bright side and not annoy anyone else with our woes.

Andy Rooney suggests—I guess in his case that would be "suggested"—that it's paradoxical that the idea of living a long life appeals to everyone, but the idea of getting older doesn't appeal to a single soul. Amen, Andy. A long life is a hazy concept. The day-to-day slog of actually getting older is a gritty reality. Spouting "You're not getting older, you're getting better" should be a punishable offense. Grape juice turns into wine, but wine eventually turns into vinegar. Case closed.

I go along with the concept that "age is just a number," but probably not for the reason intended. I feel like I'm back in grade school when you not only celebrated birthdays but also half birthdays, even quarters. Seventy-nine and three-quarters feels very different than seventy-nine. A lot of water has gone over the dam, as they say. I have friends who routinely fudge their age and make themselves younger, including one who famously forgets what she said the previous time, thus giving herself away. If I'm going to prevaricate, I would add a few years in hopes of eliciting a "Wow, you look great for your age." It's patronizing, I realize, but I still wriggle like a puppy when it's cast my way.

Others I can do without: "Seventy is the new fifty" is patently not true, and "Aging is just another word for living" is scant comfort. Anyway, I know you've heard them all. A new one for me, though, is "Wrinkles appear where smiles have been." Judging from the looks of me and my peers, we've led extraordinarily jolly lives.

There's one cliché I can get behind, though: "Old age

is not for sissies." It takes heroic courage to navigate the challenges and indignities of the process. My younger sister, as I mentioned, has had three joint replacements, a partially severed nerve that limits the use of her left hand, and double vision. She also had breast cancer but was preoccupied with physical therapy for her joints at the time and sailed through the treatment without a whimper. She's a widow living alone who still drives, though she probably shouldn't. My admiration for her is boundless, but I do miss being able to call her up and whine about my metaphorical hangnails. She has enough on her plate and doesn't need my paltry contributions. She's no sissy.

She's the most extreme example I have of rising to the occasion, but most of my pals are earning gold stars on a daily basis. Dedee, as I said, is taking care of her husband, who has had dementia for eighteen years, while also managing her COPD. John deals with a wife so weak, she rarely leaves her bed, while showing up for his regular cancer screenings. Anne makes sure her husband takes all his meds at the proper intervals so that he doesn't have another stroke, while she now walks with two canes after being hit by a car. When I was younger, my response to these circumstances would have been "Shoot me." I now know that's not an option. So far, my challenges haven't been that challenging, but they might be in the future. I'm fortunate to have strong role models and hope I'll be able to channel their inner grit.

Old age may not be for sissies, but . . . "Consider the alternative."

APPLE WATCH

I broke down and bought an Apple Watch, not for all the cool features like monitoring my steps or being able to check my email (who can read print that small anyway?). No, I bought it for the "I've fallen and I can't get up" feature. Remember those lavalieres meant to call for help in case of an oops? I gave one to my mother as a "gift," which she declared insulting but was caught wearing when she died. She didn't want to advertise being infirm, and neither do I, though the fact that I don't go up or down stairs without a railing sort of gives me away. With the Apple Watch, I've got my bases covered and even look somewhat hip should anyone bother to look. That alone is worth the price, which is fortunate, because actually telling time on it is a challenge if your readers aren't nearby. Shortly after my purchase I put it to the test by rolling out of a rather high bed and hitting the floor with an audible thud. I was shaken but fine and delighted to hear a cheerful feminine voice asking me if I was okay.

I had to retrieve my glasses to push the right button to assure her that I was but returned to bed with a smile on my face.

My life is littered with technology, most of which I can barely use but rely on for my daily existence. Our kids conduct their entire lives on their phones. I save mine for emergencies. They nimbly type away with both thumbs, while I hunt and peck with my index finger. If you are ever curious about how old someone is, which I confess I often am, wait until they pull out their phone and see if they are a thumb or a forefinger typist. You won't nail their age with complete accuracy, but you'll have a pretty good idea. What with Botox and Clairol, not to mention cosmetic surgery, age-guessing has become an inexact science. The thumbs are a helpful tool.

In addition to my phone and watch, I have a desktop computer and an iPad. I tried to use a laptop, but the keyboard aggravated the arthritis in my wrists, so I gave it to a delighted grandson to use for school. When I got my first computer, I signed up for classes at the Y but quickly found they just obscured the issue. I only want to use Word and send emails. I have no use for Excel and GarageBand, so I turned to my children, one of whom was a tech analyst at a high-powered investment bank and should have been able to address my relatively simple needs. He could, but his help seemed to come in a foreign language with no connection to the Romance languages I studied in college, and we quickly came to an impasse. His solution was to suggest, "It's intuitive." Not if you're over seventy it isn't. I try not to annoy my children, though my efforts go unrewarded, so rather than have him try to actually teach me how to use my devices, I just call him when I hit a snag. I have him on speed dial, which I'm proud to say I figured out myself. Remarkably, my calls usually go straight to voicemail.

In addition to the proliferation of devices, I have a raft of cables and chargers, some of which no longer seem to fit into any of the irritatingly small openings they are meant to. I've also accumulated chargers for items as obscure as a flashlight and curling iron. I may be old-fashioned, but what was wrong with AAs? Sure, you had to replace them, but you didn't have to plug them in all the time. When we go on a trip, I have three different chargers in my backpack—one for my iPad, one for my watch, and one for my hearing aids. "Why can't we have a universal charger?" I beg of the tech gods, knowing it's a rhetorical question. The last one I bought as an upgrade for my iPad was fifty dollars. As they say in the sport's world, "Follow the money."

I've conquered a few apps on my own—Amazon and Words With Friends—but still struggle with attaching a document to an email. I've heard that necessity is the mother of invention, but every time I light out on my own, I have to call in damage control. I remember when we adjusted the TV with rabbit ears and now find having three remotes for our current set more than a bit perplexing . . . and perhaps unnecessary. If we're flirting with commercial space travel, we ought to be able to operate the boob tube with one remote.

My mother learned to use a desktop computer when she was in her nineties, which I considered heroic. When she became bedridden and unable to get to it, I bought her an iPad, which she never got the hang of, proving that there is just so much technology us old goats can conquer. She was highly motivated, as none of her grandchildren talk on the phone, her preferred method of communication. They just text, which meant she could no longer reach them. In spite of numerous attempts, she couldn't adjust to controlling the device with her arthritic fingers and, I believe, ended up throwing it at the wall. The severely cracked screen would indicate more damage than a mere tumble out of bed would allow for. In my late seventies, I'm not far behind. I can text, but forget Instagram or Twitter. I prefer to email, as I find the urgency implicit in a text to be intrusive, but that's so old-school, my emails often don't get read. I shudder when my software needs an upgrade, knowing there will be a mandatory learning curve once it's installed and I'll feel inadequate to the task. So far, I'm holding my own, but I know there are limits to my staying power and fear the day when I can no longer keep up. It feels like the modern equivalent of being put out to pasture, and I'm really not ready to go.

PHOTO ALBUMS

They're staring at me. Twenty-four meticulously curated photo albums arranged in chronological order, waiting for me to make a mug of lemon-ginger tea and take a leisurely walk down memory lane. At least that was the point when I spent countless hours choosing the best pictures and writing clever captions. I thought looking back would make me feel all warm and fuzzy, basking in the glow of a life well lived. The albums were meant to spark fond memories of the truly wonderful life I've enjoyed and elicit a satisfied smile in my later years. I was meant to be happy and grateful for the experiences and people that are chronicled. I was meant to be okay with the fact that these memories were in the past and that I wouldn't be making many more new ones.

It doesn't seem to be working that way. I pull out no. 8 to find a picture of my daughter, Courtney, as a six-year-old on her league-winning soccer team. Instead of reliving the excitement we shared when she brought home her trophy, I lament the one game I missed and how annoyed I used to get when her practices overlapped with dinner. Ditto when I see my grandson Brooks in his Jolly Jumper in a later album. I remember him being smiley and energetic as he bobbed, but I also remember being relieved he was entertained so that I could clean up the kitchen. Rather than comforting memories, these feel like missed opportunities.

I've heard of people expressing content at the end of their lives but suspect they're putting lipstick on the pig. We're too flawed as a species not to have amassed a boatload of blunders that we can't help but regret when the sand is getting low in the upper part of the hour glass. Perhaps if you don't have children, you have a lighter load, but if you do—and most of us do—the regrets are weighed in tonnage.

I caught wind of the endless guilt trip that parenting becomes the first day in the hospital after my daughter was born. She was howling in the bassinet the nurses had put by my bed so that we could "bond," and I had a horrific headache caused no doubt by the two days of labor I had endured to bring her into this world. It was foreboding. I rolled her to the nurse's station to explain the situation and suggest they take her back to the nursery so that I could sleep. They turned on me with looks so withering, they didn't have to open their mouths. I rolled her back to my room in excruciating awareness that I'd flunked my first test as a mother. I get a psychosomatic headache just thinking about it.

But parenthood is only one area of potential regret. There's the whole minefield about your relationship with your own parents. If you had easygoing parents who had the consideration to die peacefully in their sleep, you can skip this section. I did not. My mother lived well into her nineties, growing evermore hard of hearing (a euphemism for deaf) and mostly bedridden. She lived hundreds of miles from my siblings and I, which while not calculated to make us feel guilty, certainly succeeded. I dreaded my visits beforehand and felt even worse when they were over. When she was still capable of getting out of bed, she could use a desktop computer to email her kids, grands, and great-grands. Once she couldn't get out of bed, that avenue of communication was cut off, and talking to her on the phone was like "talking to a deaf wall"—an expression of hers that never made sense to me but does paint a picture. In a gesture of what I considered heroic generosity, I bought her the aforementioned iPad and trekked to her house to teach her how to use it. (If you read the previous essay, you know how this turns out.) OMG. First of all, her hands weren't nimble enough to navigate the touch screen. Secondly, the print was too small, and when enlarged to a readable size, had about three words on the screen. Thirdly, she couldn't understand my instructions and began to view me as an instrument of torture. I now own an extra (severely cracked) iPad and a great sadness that I wasn't able to help her stay in touch with the outside world.

The beat goes on. I regret excluding Martha Brouse from our neighborhood gang, I'm contrite that I lied to my fifth-grade teacher that my parents were away and couldn't be contacted about the lipstick I was wearing to class with their permission, I cringe to think about the day I organized my pals to constantly drop their books on the floor to fluster our middle school history teacher . . . though I do so with a grin. And, while I'm cringing, one of my worst nightmares is a parade of some of the lads I dated rather than staying home with my younger sibs. But that's a topic for another day.

So, the tea will have to wait until I have someone to share the albums with. When another person is looking over my shoulder, the good times take center stage. I can smile while showing my granddaughters the picture of my husband and me kayaking in Maine when we had no idea what we were doing, or while trotting out the photos of our high school graduations. I will be filled with amusing stories, not lugubrious regrets. Life is short but generally sweet.

I have the pictures to prove it.

CARBON FOOTPRINT

I have a recurring nightmare that I'm sitting in a field surrounded by everything I own. The field is littered—there is no other adjective that conveys the chaos—with things I once deemed necessary that now seem excessive. There's a big Cuisinart and a small Cuisinart for tasks that my highly sharpened knives (because—ta-da!—I own a knife sharpener) can handle. There is a ricer to make perfect mashed potatoes, which we used to make at Thanksgiving but now have catered. There is a set of my mother's china, a set of my grandmother's china, and the set of exquisite Herend china I received as wedding gifts and own every piece of—from the soup tureen (unused) to nut dishes (also virgin). That, too, is only used at Thanksgiving. I could give it to my daughter-in-law, who coincidentally has the same

pattern, but she doesn't even use hers for Thanksgiving—
they come to our house. Why should it take up space at
her house rather than ours?

When was the last time I wore that fuchsia silk dress
and jacket I thought so perfect for weddings? Looks a
tad bright now. Or the little black dress you could dress
up or down? Truth be told, I don't go much of anywhere
these days, and the places I do go require nothing more
than white jeans in summer and black jeans in winter.
The women's magazines suggest you get rid of anything
you haven't worn in the last three years, but some of these
clothes feel too valuable to part with. Which brings me
to the shoes. I could buy a small car, a Yugo, perhaps (if
they still make them) with the cash tied up in names you
would recognize, but I refuse to divulge. I'm pleading the
Fifth. I would need a cane to steady myself if I wore those
heels—which would seriously ruin the look—but I can't
bring myself to give them away.

At my hypothetical estate sale, the shoes would get
snapped up in a heartbeat, but what happens to the rest of
this mess? My siblings and I filled up an entire dumpster
with things we couldn't get rid of when we cleaned out my
mother's house. She had kept the glass vases from every
flower arrangement she had ever been gifted, had drawers
full of rusting knives, and had stockpiled enough plastic
take-out containers from the deli to open a deli of her

own. So far I'm not that far gone, but I do have a bunch of plastic cutlery all done up in cellophane that I didn't need because I brought my salad home from Panera. I'd like to give them back, but I'm sure there are hygiene laws that prevent such a rational move.

So here I am, surrounded by things most people won't want. The kids will take the jewelry because it has some value, even if too out-of-date to actually wear, but what about the demilunes and highboys? They were valuable once, too, but are now tainted by being brown. I could make the argument that as antiques, they'll come back, but I know I'll get polite nods, and the family heirlooms will hit the chopping block soon after we're gone. If I add in all the detergent and Clorox and even water that has been expended maintaining this pile, I see a carbon footprint the size of a *T. Rex*. I'm deeply ashamed, yet I just bought another gray hoodie because it has the logo of my grandson's college. And think I should replace my bath towels. Fluffy ones are a weakness. Amazon beckons. I remember looking at the bizarre array of items in my mother's house and wondering how it happened. At ninety-six and the last survivor of both her and my father's families, she'd had plenty of time to amass such disparate items as a Coromandel screen that my grandparents had brought back from prewar China and a matched set of candlesticks shaped like pineapples. It was a road map of her life, interesting from a sociological standpoint, but most of it useless. I came home from there vowing not to leave our kids with a similar mess and, in fact, did find homes for an unused soup pot and some extra outdoor furniture. Even so, I still have two sets of demitasse cups with accompanying monogrammed silver spoons that are useful merely as decor in our glass-fronted cabinets. I remember how grown up I felt receiving them as wedding gifts, which was ridiculous even then. My parents were more likely to toss back a brandy after dinner than sip a demitasse. They were mere decoration for their generation too.

I wake from the dream committed to dealing responsibly with the pile but become overwhelmed by the task. I make the odd stab by giving my granddaughters some nice jewelry my mother had given me at their age, but these are token attempts and don't really move the needle. The pile is barely reduced, and if I'm honest, I'll probably follow in my mother's footsteps and just kick the can down the road. Guess I better leave a stipend for dumpsters in my will.

WHAT COULD GO WRONG?

"What could go wrong?" A question just begging for trouble. The answer at any age is "everything," but the odds go up with each passing year. The world is fraught with stumbling blocks for us seniors. We need such a staggering amount of gear to navigate even a simple outing, it's almost impossible not to forget something. I have a friend who uses the catchy mantra "spectacles, testicles" to remind her to think through everything she will need for whatever perils await. I would need something more specific like "Car keys, driver's license, credit cards, cell phone," which is lacking in poetic cachet. Even then, I'm sure I would leave something crucial behind. AARP advertises a vest with multiple pockets for necessities, which just screams *senior citizen* and, fully loaded, might be hazardous for those of us with osteopenia.

A recent weekend with friends underscored the difficulty of getting it right. My husband thoughtfully put his wallet and keys into the pair of khakis he deemed perfect for the trip, then proceeded to wear another pair. Fortunately, I was covered on both fronts but felt uneasy that only one of us was armed. Next up was our attempt to pick up the rental car reserved in our friend Mary's name. Seems she had left *her* license behind in some mysterious item she called the "fish bag." We feared for the fish. Luckily, her husband had *his* license, and after some complex negotiating with Hertz (since the reservation was in her name), we were good to go with him as our pilot. We were feeling pleased with our ability to pivot until Mary asked where the boat bag might be. This was to be a leafing escapade in Maine, where warm clothes were de rigueur, and theirs were in this bag. After a flurry of frantic phone calls, the bag was found to have been left in the car of the person who took Mary and her husband to the airport and not retrievable. My husband and I, recent Floridians, had come equipped for the Arctic, so we patted ourselves on the back for being overprepared and shared our gear.

So far, I had escaped leaving anything behind and was feeling secretly smug, but my arrogance proved fleeting. Emerging from a shower with freshly washed hair, I discovered that I didn't have my curling brush, my electric curling iron, or a brush of any sort. My hair is three inches long max, but to achieve the sufficiently unmatronly coif I deem necessary to counteract the effects of going gray, I need an arsenal of equipment. I panicked. We were meeting up with some old (in both senses of the word) high school pals, and I wanted to look my best. Drip-dry was not an option. I had two Velcro rollers (always on hand for volumizing the bangs), which I ingeniously used in place of the curling brush along with lots and lots of product. The result, while not runway worthy, was passable, and the breezy day helped me look like windswept was what I was after anyway.

As the day progressed, my husband lost his room key, I discovered I didn't have my phone charger, we entered the wrong destination in Google Maps, and my husband was without a razor. Our friends left their sunglasses somewhere, and between us, we only had about twenty dollars in cash. In all fairness, we hadn't been on a trip since the beginning of Covid and were out of practice, but we had undeniably lost more than a step or two. I could excuse the phone charger. I go through life with a cell phone, an iPad, and an Apple Watch. They all have to be charged daily, and they all have different chargers. Easy to leave one behind, right?

We collectively felt diminished and vulnerable. We could work around the problems, view them courageously as challenges, and try to laugh it off, though it was decidedly gallows humor. But it was impossible not to be afraid of the trend. We were clearly not as sharp as we once were and had to consider that at some point in the not-too-distant future, we wouldn't be capable of such a caper at all. It was sobering.

We vowed to be more thoughtful on our next adventure, tried to chalk this up as a learning experience, merely a one-time oops, but I think we knew we were kidding ourselves. Next time, I'll make lists, plan in advance, and pack with intention ... but I will do it with a nagging sense of inadequacy and the knowledge that the answer to the question "What can go wrong?" is "Everything."

ELEPHANT IN THE ROOM

A supplement just arrived from Amazon that has me stumped. I don't remember ordering it but know from past experience that I probably read that it has life-extending properties. I can Google it, of course, and will, but I think it's time to put the brakes on my snake oil habit. I don't take many prescription drugs but am vulnerable to the siren call of supplements and routinely add a handful of the supposedly magic herbs to my morning cocktail. The last time I gave our doctor a list of my supplements, he shook his head and declared he had no idea what most of them did but liked the results, so he suggested that I keep on swallowing.

I have it on good authority that the average senior (could there be such a thing?) takes five prescription pills a day. It's the rare octogenarian who doesn't have "issues." I have osteopenia and advancing arthritis. My husband has a pacemaker and a rare, but so far manageable, blood cancer. Things we can live with. But—big "buts" abound in later life—we know there is more to come, and it's tricky "living" under the threat of mortality. It's a buzzkill, but death is the elephant in the room. Impossible to avoid.

I'm a big fan of books like the ones Oprah specializes in that boil down complex philosophical ideas into sound bites, so that I can glean the essence without actually plowing through the text. I particularly like Pierre Teilhard de Chardin, who claims that we are "spiritual beings having a human experience." Many of Oprah's gurus address "end of life," as they pleasantly refer to our inevitable demise. I've pored over their insights intently and come away with the sense that while their language may be more florid than mine, they are just as much in the dark.

It's a scary place to be. I thought that addressing it head-on would take the sting out of my questions, but I'm left with a hanging chad. I claim to be an agnostic, which Wikipedia tells me means that I find existence unknowable. That should quell the debate, right? It doesn't. I want to know at breakfast what we're having for dinner, so I damn well want to know where I'm going once the lights go out. Finer minds than mine have failed to figure it out, so it's arrogance on my part to think I might succeed. But once you open that Pandora's box, you simply can't close it. You can only work around the edges and live in the present. Oprah's gurus do come in handy there. They've convinced me to meditate (badly, but I'm assured that's how it's done), spend time in nature, do one task at a time, and most importantly, express gratitude. I roll my eyeballs at the thought of a gratitude journal but confess I keep a list on my bedside table to force myself to keep score. I also have GRATITUDE IS A PRACTICE pinned to my bulletin board and no longer view it as woo-woo wisdom. I can't always achieve my desired zen state, but I no longer endlessly ruminate and, as a result, find I'm experiencing more joy.

There is a lot to be said for carpe diem. It may be all we get.

GRATITUDE IS A PRACTICE

Research indicates that gratitude really does increase with practice. I try. Some days I confess, though, that my gratitude tends toward being grateful I'm not Jan, taking care of a husband with Alzheimer's, or Karen, going through radiation treatment. It speaks badly of my character, but I have a hard time getting a positive jolt out of just being able to get out of bed in the morning. I know people who do and feel ashamed that I'm not one of them.

I've read from credible sources that the majority of people over seventy-five are happier with their lives than they were at fifty-five. The idea is that they no longer have the responsibility of caring for children or chasing a career or worrying about aging parents. But come on, it's the rare geezer who doesn't have challenges—heart palpitations, osteoporosis, cataracts, arthritis. And those are the relatively benign ones. I'm humbled by the people who can joke during chemo. I'd like to think I'd be one of them but suspect otherwise.

I recently took a trip down I-95 in South Florida, which is five lanes of bumper-to-bumper traffic with tricky off-ramps that allow monster trucks to whiz by on the right at death-defying speeds. In my forties I would have been frightened but in control and relatively safe. At seventy-nine and a quarter, I'm panicked and dangerous. My reflexes aren't what they once were, but it's my shot nerves that are the real problem. I've never been an overly confident driver, but aging is doing a real number on my dwindling reserves.

"How can I be happy with such limitations?" I ask myself.

"Gratitude," I hear my irritating inner voice whisper. "Look around at all you have."

It sounds suspiciously like the guilt trip my parents used to lay on us about the starving Armenians so that we would eat my mother's dreadful tomato aspic.

That inner voice is annoying . . . because she's right. She's given me the answer to the question but not the tools to implement it, at least not to the degree these "happy" seniors report. In truth, their "happiness" seems a bit simpleminded to me. I can be grateful that I can walk around our block unassisted but know the day I can't is in the wings. I'm grateful that I can still drive, but a jury of my peers—and certainly my family—are poised to pounce should I leave my keys lying around. My mother always claimed she would "die with her boots on," which made her feel invincible. She actually died barefoot in critical need of a pedicure. Gratitude and reality feel like opposing forces. Don't get me wrong. I believe that gratitude is essential, but reality has to be part of the equation too. It's a tricky balancing act, and I feel a bit wobbly.

THE GRANDS

Back from a visit with my grandson Brooks at college, I'm high on youthful optimism and enthusiasm. It beats a shot of vitamin B_{12}. I envy the professors who get to inhale this electric energy on a daily basis. Unlike high school, the slackers are free to cut class with no consequences, so I envision the professors surrounded by the eager and engaged. What a rush.

"I hope you'll come back again," my grandson said as a goodbye, which was music to my ears.

"He can't possibly mean it," my husband suggested, fearful that I might try to cancel our flight.

I'm skeptical myself. My grandson has been raised with the impeccable manners my Nashville daughter-in-law instills and may just have just been being polite. Nevertheless, he's on record as asking for it.

My husband used to complain that at sit-down dinners, the women just wanted to talk about their children. Fortunately for him, we are no longer invited to such functions. With age presumably comes wisdom, and spending more hours in the kitchen than it takes to devour the meal makes little sense to us aging hostesses. Nibbles will do, and even they garner less attention than the wine. As a result, he is spared news of the game-winning touchdown young Henry scored or the rave review little Karen received for her piano recital. He can also avoid what I call "grandmother gushing," which is way more intense than reporting on children ever was. How can it not be? Our grandchildren are our children with no strings attached. They're generally on their best behavior around us, and we don't have to experience the illusion-busting reality of actually raising them.

It's a win-win relationship. The benefits to both sides are well documented, but I feel they're weighted in my favor. I have the privilege of being involved with seven grands, all of whom contribute something unique to my life. From Luke I've learned to almost understand football—his passion. Gracie has motivated me to read Harry Potter, though not all of them. Ellie keeps me up to date on middle school fashion. Poppy pointed out all the important lines in the movie *The Princess Bride*, thus allowing me to quote them at will and sound uncharacteristically in the know. That's only four, but I'll stop. I was so busy teaching my children, I failed to learn the many things they had to offer me.

The learning goes deeper than these superficial examples. I see them as fully formed people and accept them in ways I could never accept my children. They aren't reflections of me, after all . . . well, maybe when Ward aces a math test or Francie scores a hockey goal. I can take some credit for their accomplishments but precious little for their character. It's liberating.

I don't see them as much as I would like but suspect that if I did, I would find it exhausting, and the novelty that keeps the relationship exciting would pall. It would become a lot like . . . sigh . . . having children. And I'm sure that whatever they find in me (which I sense diminishing at a rapid rate with the teenagers) would disappear completely. I would become like their parents. So, I love them with an urgency I never felt with my kids. Our time together is going to be so very short—from my perspective anyway.

I'm planning my return trip to Brooks's college with the eerie sense that a lot can happen in the intervening months and the visit might not take place. I'm at the age where the cliché about not buying green bananas is starting to make sense, if still too corny to articulate out loud. It reminds me to "Strike while the iron is hot," Midwestern wisdom passed on from *my* grandmother. At dinner on our visit, I asked Brooks what he remembered about our times together, which turned out to be precious little. I know he can't possibly remember that he took his first steps in my kitchen, but I'm heartbroken that he doesn't remember being my buddy the first time he went snorkeling. It drives home the inherent inequality in the relationship. He's central to my life. I'm a blip in his. As is our tradition, Brooks and I say "I love you" in closing, and I think it's genuine—or as genuine as it can be for an eighteen-year-old boy. He takes my presence for granted. I know his is a gift.

ACCEPTING HELP

I was mumbling to myself at Publix. You know, something along the lines of, "Don't forget the low-fat yogurt again, you idiot," which caused an attentive stock boy to ask if I needed help. Well, cosmically, of course I do, but I had this one under control—and you would think in South Florida, with about 30 percent of the population over seventy, mumbling would go unnoticed. It brought me up short, being asked if I needed help. So far, my need for assistance is confined to small things—opening up ketchup bottles, replacing light bulbs that require a ladder, reading the small print on my phone, and all things technological. When my husband's executive assistant moved with us to Florida, I suggested she join a support group for caregivers. I was being facetious at the time, but we lean on her more and more, and the handwriting is on the wall. I watched my mother need more help as she aged and knew how much she hated it. One of her last acts of defiance was throwing her hearing aids at the wall. They were tangible evidence of the dependence she loathed.

My sister traveled through an airport this Christmas in a wheelchair after taking a nasty fall that cracked her pelvis. The year prior she had taken another nasty fall, severing a nerve near her neck, which has compromised the use of her left hand. In a short period of time, she went from being a fiercely independent widow to being someone who needed occasional "assistance." This is a woman who foxhunted at breakneck speed and was sought after as a doubles tennis partner for her wicked crosscourt slice. She could bushhog a field, ride the jittery mare that frightened others, or drive a group of teens to the Green Day concert that terrified other parents. She didn't go in the mosh pit, but I suspect that's only because she was the designated driver. She was the person who dispensed help, not the one who needed it.

Florida Scott-Maxwell, author, psychologist, and all-around wise (and old) woman, notes the importance of being "fierce with reality" as we age. I get all chuffed up and, well, *fierce* reading those words but lose air like a popped balloon when called into battle. At the end of my mother's life, she needed help getting out of bed, bathing herself, changing her pj's. A world-class cook, she was reduced to whatever her caregivers could nuke in the microwave. In her prime she was described as strong-willed, independent, a force to be reckoned with. At her fiftieth birthday party she announced to the celebrants that from now on, she was "going to do whatever she damned well pleased," a pronouncement that surprised no one, as we all felt it was no change in policy. She was a woman capable of looking reality in the eye and staring it down. She could be fierce, but at the end of the day, even she had to accept help.

If life grants us a second or third act, we're all going to need assistance. The key is accepting it, particularly before we hurt ourselves or someone else. It isn't hard to understand that you need physical therapy after a hip replacement (few of us nearing eighty aren't at least partially bionic), but it's considerably more challenging to admit you should use Uber to go out to dinner—and not just because you plan to have a second martini. Ironically, asking for help feels like losing control, when it's actually empowering. I can pretend I don't need help reaching the book on the top shelf and decide I don't want to read it anyway, or risk breaking my neck going up the step stool. Or (best option) ... I can be smart—bordering on wise—by asking my six-foot-three grandson to get it for me.

We recently learned that friends have sold their beautiful retirement home to move into high-rise assisted living. "They're so young," we gasp, realizing, of course, that only a seventy-nine-year-old could consider a seventy-seven-year-old young.

"She does need help with her oxygen tank," we rationalize, to absolve us from making the same decision and completely miss the point. They're taking control of their future, not losing it. Few of us are nearly as prudent. The majority of us will wait until a fractured hip or failing eyesight forces us into some sort of assisted situation, often with diminished options. Close friends waited until both partners were so incapacitated, no facility would take them, so they're stuck at home with full-time, exorbitantly expensive care and very anxious children. We would all like to die at home in our own beds (preferably in our sleep), but the odds are against it.

I talk a good game but admit I'm one of the tribe that hopes to gut it out until absolutely necessary. I've witnessed the downside of that attitude and ought to know better. My mother chose to stay in her home with a rotating staff that took care of her immediate physical needs but did little to engage her mind. She had outlived most of her friends, so the TV became her daily companion, switching from golf, which she could no longer play, to the cooking channel, although she no longer cooked and barely ate. Tell me aging isn't funny. All three of her children lived far away, and although we stayed in touch by phone, her lack of hearing made those calls frustrating and unsatisfactory to both parties. I think she would have had more of a life in what she disparagingly called an "old-age home," but she wasn't buying it, and apparently, I don't see it as an option either . . . at least not yet.

I remember watching Arthur Godfrey on the wonderful days I was allowed to stay home "sick" and watch daytime TV on the couch. He had an oft-repeated axiom, "Too soon old, too late smart," that stuck in my brain. It didn't make much sense to me in grade school, but it has doggedly remained in my mind, as if the universe is trying to warn me to wise up. I'd like to think I'm listening, and believe I will at some point, but not today.

LETTING GO

My closest friend in grief and life, Dedee, told me that she thought the death of her son was meant to teach her about impermanence. It sounded philosophical and Buddhist to me at the time. I had just lost my daughter and was more prone to thinking it was meant to reinforce the idea that life was unfair, an irony my daughter would have appreciated given how often I tried to her teach that life lesson. As you might imagine, it drove her crazy and did nothing to assuage her anger when she was relegated to second-string hockey despite her superior stick skill or given a B on a paper about anorexia that she had slaved to make A material. Dedee's reasoning felt spiritual and enlightened, but I just couldn't get there. I thought I had already embraced impermanence. I knew I had to trade my car in after five years, saw my hair lose its "natural color," lost my ancient gardenias in spite of my diligent pruning and fertilizing. I knew things died, but I knew it intellectually, not viscerally. Dedee was talking about feeling it on a gut level.

When hospice was called in for my ninety-six-year-old mother, I watched her battle fiercely for life even in a morphine-induced coma. I fear I'm my mother's daughter. I'm finding it difficult to let go, yet aging requires it. A central teaching of Buddhism is that the art of life is embracing every moment and letting go as those moments pass. I'd make a terrible monk. My friends are more evolved. Jenny can no longer play tennis but has become a dedicated gardener. Susan can no longer hike but drives to different locations each day to keep her walks interesting. They're finding the open door behind the closed one. I'm still rattling the lock.

My understanding of Buddhism is superficial at best, but I believe one tenet is that our suffering is caused by attachment, the desire to have and control. It claims there is a way out, but the Noble Eightfold Path looks like it requires more time than I have left.

My mother let go unwillingly. I'm going to try to be smarter and make it easier on myself. I'll need to start small, convince myself to look past the stains the dog has permanently imprinted on the bedspread, forget about fixing the dents in my car, as there are bound to be more. I might even be able to meditate my way past wearing high heels. It won't be easy. The desire to hang on is strong, but it's pretty exhausting and, at the end of the day, a losing battle. I'll try to find the comfort in *om*. I'll try to smell the roses. I'll try to emulate my dog and live in the moment like she does.

I'll try to let go.

DUE DATE

Some days I feel past my shelf life—fit for consumption but past my prime and headed for the dumpster. I take deep breaths, drink buckets of caffeine, stretch my quads, stand in the sun. But something is off. The mind says, "You go girl," but the body answers, "Are you kidding?"

Seventy is definitely *not* the new fifty. At fifty I could play tennis four times a week, keep up with the front row in Bikram yoga, and hop off our boat to secure dock lines. I couldn't keep up with my son hiking, but then maybe I never could. I was a slower version of my former self but not a different one. I had to take an occasional break to catch my breath. Now I take a break because further effort is simply impossible. The literature suggests being grateful for the functioning I do have, along with encouraging blurbs about fellow seniors who have made peace with their infirmities. You know, the woman with arthritis who gives up knitting baby blankets but discovers a passion for aqua jogging . . . provided the pool is over eighty-five degrees. I consider it elder shaming. How can you not miss the person you once were?

I secretly don't think you can, but I try to keep that to myself, as it comes off as whiny, which is as off-putting in an old person as it is in a toddler. Plus, whom do I have left to complain to? Marion has Parkinson's. Ann is only three years into remission from pancreatic cancer. Cathy's son has a brain tumor. They would listen to the complaints about my frozen neck, but only because they have good manners. Their concerns far outweigh mine, and we all know it. I know better than to press the issue. At moments like this I miss my mom, who was duty bound to hear me out. Her advice was always to have a stiff upper lip, which wasn't exactly helpful, but I did know she cared.

Physical limitations are just part of the equation. It's hard to feel relevant. I can go watch my granddaughter play soccer but can no longer kick the ball around with her. I can listen to my grandson's experience at college but am too far out of the loop to offer insight. The bereavement group I facilitated for years has kept me on as a guest, but it's a courtesy. They want to acknowledge my past contribution but also hope I'll remain silent. It's no longer my gig. I need to relinquish my shelf space.

My husband is fond of railing at the aging politicians on TV, accusing them of being out of touch. I won't name names, but you know who they are. In theory, age should confer wisdom, and I think I do understand the world better at seventy-nine than I did at fifty-nine. I just don't know where to go with that knowledge. I think even Aristotle would have a hard time gaining cred in our youth-centric culture.

I gripe about loads of laundry and meal prep, but those tasks give structure to my day and a sense—albeit minor—of purpose. I check in on my sister regularly and on my friends probably more often than they would care to be scrutinized. I'm careful about calling the kids—I text first to make sure it's a good time. The grands don't talk on the phone, so I text supportive (and brief) messages with no expectation of a response. I'm not confined to a BarcaLounger yet. I still have a life, not just an existence, but my due date is right around the corner.

Fact is, I'm lucky to have been on the shelf at all.

NOSTALGIA

I thought I'd look back fondly on my life. It's been a privileged and a full one after all, but I'm finding reminiscing to be painful. As I hope I've conveyed through the previous essays, I'm a fairly upbeat individual and generally see the humor in life, but these days, my memories are tinged with more than a little sadness and regret. Not just the big, obvious ones, though there are plenty of those—not finishing college, getting divorced, losing the finals to Innis Arden in a tiebreaker. Even the sweet, little memories, like how my son, Michael, used to stamp his feet in the shower water after our parent-child swim lessons at the Y, bring a pang. He couldn't shower by himself at home, and being allowed to stand under all that water as we rinsed off the chlorine caused him to dance with delight. It was an exuberant, happy time. Why the heavy heart?

I hate those essays where the author quotes the dictionary, but here goes. *Nostalgia*—the number-one definition in my *Webster's Ninth New Collegiate Dictionary* is "homesickness." It goes on to say it's "a wistful yearning for return to some past period or irrecoverable condition." If asked to pick A or B on the SAT, I would have gone with B, the wistful yearning, but homesickness paints a more intense picture. For me it's very akin to the desperate longing for my old familiar bed every time my life has changed direction, even when the direction was positive.

For many of us nostalgia becomes an unwanted companion when our kids flee the nest. You don't miss the noise and the mess and, in our house at least, the constant squabbling, but you ache for the connection. The kids are still part of your life, but they're no longer central to it. It leaves an abyss. At that point you can still sit down and reminisce happily though. Remember when Courtney hid her boyfriend Glen in the basement for a week? When the diminutive cop dragged six-foot-two Michael home from the pool he and his friends had broken into? We chortle happily because there's still so much ahead.

I'm in reasonably good shape physically and think I have all my marbles, though you, dear reader, will have to be the judge of that. Pushing eighty, there isn't all that much runway ahead, which tends to inform even the happiest of times and, unfortunately, seems to compromise memories. Even though it's sometimes painful, I'll keep taking trips down memory lane. I'll continue to dredge up the day I went to Courtney's fourth-grade classroom and discovered the skirts I'd forced her to wear stuffed in her desk and remember the time Michael was in the loo from too much partying when his name was called for his Phi Beta Kappa pin. They will make me smile . . . but not laugh out loud like they used to.

I like the idea of a life well lived and think I've squeezed that lemon dry in my own idiosyncratic way. At summer camp we were taught to leave our campsite better than we found it, a value I've tried to live by, and I think I've succeeded on my small playing field. I've earned my memories and treasure them. They do make me homesick though.

YOU HAVE TO LAUGH

My daughter, Courtney, was killed at age twenty-two in an automobile accident when I was forty-eight. I thought I wouldn't survive, and for a while it was touch and go. But the will to live is a powerful force, and it wouldn't let go of me. Years later, when I had my feet back under me, I had the privilege of facilitating groups of bereaved parents, which helped me develop a deep respect for the resilience of the human spirit. I began to see us as plants that will grow toward the sun given a chance.

The first time I laughed after my daughter's death, I was shocked. How could I find something funny in the wake of such a life-changing loss? I think her dog, whom we had adopted, had hidden under an azalea bush to get away from our resident mutt and was covered with pink flowers. I had to laugh. It was liberating and a fork in the road. Something inside me relaxed, and I started to have a life, not just an existence. In the twenty-five years I ran grief groups, I watched similar shifts take place with others. The capacity to be amused is restorative. Our group sessions were filled with more laughter than I would have anticipated. Life, after all, is plenty absurd.

So ... laugh when you can and look for reasons to smile. As my therapist friends remind me, you can't control events, only your reaction to them. I don't think it's quite that simple. There are emotions that come on like a tsunami and are out of your control. But the light is usually also there somewhere, if only faintly. It's terrifying to grow old, but it's also pretty funny. Laughter is the only response to calling in your grandson to open the jam jar or having your son on speed dial for technological emergencies. I don't find my husband's lymphoma diagnosis amusing but do have fun bantering with the nurses during his treatments. I might be a Pollyanna—at least a little bit—but it's serving me well. I know my excessive workouts may not make me live longer, as my mother likes to tell me, but they make me feel better along the way. I view laughter and aging similarly.

You don't *have* to laugh, of course, but once you start, it becomes a habit.

ABOUT THE AUTHOR

Susan Evans has crossed the Rubicon and is now an official octogenarian. She lives most of the year in South Florida, where it's easy to find things to laugh about—iguanas that fall out of trees when the temperature drops, doctors' offices that lock their doors during lunch so that elderly patients don't linger to socialize, beaches covered with underdressed retirees, and a certain politician who will remain nameless. Loss is ever present, but so is laughter.

Printed in the USA
CPSIA information can be obtained
at www.ICGtesting.com
JSHW022109110724
66103JS00005B/140/J

9 781951 568429